THE GERMAN WHITE-BOOK

(Only authorized translation)

How Russia and her Ruler betrayed Germany's confidence and thereby caused the European War

WITH THE ORIGINAL TELEGRAMS

AND NOTES.

Druck und Verlag: Liebheit & Thiesen, Berlin.

Price 40 Pf.

Foreign Office,
Berlin, August 1914.

On June 28th the Austro-Hungarian successor to the throne, Arch-Duke Franz Ferdinand, and his wife, the Duchess of Hohenberg, were assassinated by a member of a band of servian conspirators. The investigation of the crime through the Austro-Hungarian authorities has yielded the fact that the conspiracy against the life of the Arch-Duke and successor to the throne was prepared and abetted in Belgrade with the cooperation of Servian officials, and executed with arms from the Servian State arsenal. This crime must have opened the eyes of the entire civilized world, not only in regard to the aims of the Servian policies directed against the conservation and integrity of the Austro-Hungarian monarchy, but also concerning the criminal means which the pan-Serb propaganda in Servia had no hesitation in employing for the achievement of these aims.

The goal of these policies was the gradual revolutionizing and final separation of the south-easterly districts from the Austro-Hungarian monarchy and their union with Servia. This direction of Servias policy has not been altered in the least in spite of the repeated and solemn declarations of Servia in which it vouchsafed a change in these policies toward Austria-Hungary as well as the cultivation of good and neighborly relations.

In this manner for the third time in the course of the last 6 years Servia has led Europe to the brink of a world-war.

It could only do this because it believed itself supported in its intentions by Russia.

Russia soon after the events brought about by the Turkish revolution of 1908, endeavored to found a union of the Balcan states under Russian patronage and directed against the existence of Turkey. This union which succeeded in 1911 in driving out Turkey from a greater part of her European possessions, collapsed over the question of the distribution of spoils. The Russian policies were not dismayed over this failure. According to the idea of the Russian statesmen a new Balcan union under Russian patronage should be called into existence, headed no longer against Turkey, now dislodged from the Balcan, but against the existence of the Austro-Hungarian monarchy. It was the idea that Servia should cede to Bulgaria those parts of Macedonia which it had received during the last Balcan war, in exchange for Bosnia and the Herzegovina which were to be taken from Austria. To oblige Bulgaria to fall in with this plan it was to be isolated, Roumania attached to Russia with the aid of French propaganda, and Servia promised Bosnia and the Herzegovina.

Under these circumstances it was clear to Austria that it was not compatible with the dignity and the spirit of self-preservation of the monarchy to view idly any longer this agitation across the border. The Imperial and Royal Government appraised Germany of this conception and asked for our opinion. With all our heart we were able to agree with our allys estimate of the situation, and assure him that any action considered necessary to end the movement in Servia directed against the conservation of the monarchy would meet with our approval.

We were perfectly aware that a possible warlike attitude of Austria-Hungary against Servia might bring Russia upon the field, and that it might therefore involve us in a war, in accordance with our duty as allies. We could not, however, in these vital interests of Austria-Hungary, which were at stake, advise our ally to take a yielding attitude not compatible with his dignity, nor deny him our assistance in these trying days. We could do this all the less as our own interests were menaced trough the continued Serb agitation. If the Serbs continued with the aid of Russia and France to menace the existence of Austria-Hungary, the gradual collapse of Austria and the subjection of all the Slavs under one Russian sceptre would be the consequence, thus making untenable the position of the Teutonic race in Central Europe. A morally weakened Austria under the pressure of Russian pan-slavism would be no longer an ally on whom we could count and in whom we could have confidence, as we must be able to have, in view of the ever more menacing attitude of our easterly and westerly neighbors. We, therefore, permitted Austria a completely free hand in her action towards Servia but have not participated in her preparations.

Austria chose the method of presenting to the Servian Government a note, in which the direct connection between the murder at Sarajevo and the pan-Serb movement, as not only countenanced but actively supported by the Servian Government, was explained, and in which a complete cessation of this agitation, as well as a punishment of the guilty, was requested. At the same time Austria-Hungary demanded as necessary guarantee for the accomplishment of her desire the participation of some Austrian officials in the preliminary examination on Servian territory and the final dissolution of the pan-Serb societies agitating against Austria-Hungary. The Imperial and Royal Government gave a period of 48 hours for the unconditional acceptance of its demands.

The Servian Government started the mobilization of its army one day after the transmission of the Austro-Hungarian note.

As after the stipulated date the Servian Government rendered a reply which, though complying in some points with the conditions of Austria-Hungary, yet showed in all essentials the endeavor through procrastination and new negotiations to escape from the just demands of the monarchy, the latter discontinued her diplomatic relations with Servia without indulging in further negotiations or accepting further Servian assurances, whose value, to its loss, she had sufficiently experienced.

From this moment Austria was in fact in a state of war with Servia, which it proclaimed officially on the 28th of July by declaring war.

From the beginning of the conflict we assumed the position that there were here concerned the affairs of Austria alone, which it would have to settle with Servia. We therefore directed our efforts toward the localizing of the war, and toward convincing the other powers that Austria-Hungary had to appeal to arms in justifiable self-defence, forced upon her by the conditions. We emphatically took the position that no civilized country possessed the right to stay the arm of Austria in this struggle with barbarism and political crime, and to shield the Servians see exhibits 1 & 2. against their just punishment. In this sense we instructed our representatives with the foreign powers.

Simultaneously the Austro - Hungarian Government communicated to the Russian Government that the step undertaken against Servia implied merely a defensive measure against the Serb agitation, but that Austria-Hungary must of necessity demand guarantees for a continued friendly behavior of Servia towards the monarchy. Austria-Hungary had no intention whatsoever to shift the balance of power see exhibit 3. in the Balcan.

In answer to our declaration that the German Government desired, and aimed at, a localization of the conflict, both the French and the English Governments promised an action in the same direction. But these endeavors did not succeed in preventing the interposition of Russia in the Austro-Servian disagreement.

The Russian Government submitted an official communiqué on July 24th, according to which Russia could not possibly remain indifferent in the Servio-Austrian conflict. The same was declared by the Russian Secretary of Foreign Affairs, M. Sasonow, to the German Ambassador,

Count Pourtalés, in the afternoon of July 26th. The German
Government declared again, through its Ambassador at
St. Petersburg, that Austria-Hungary had no desire for
conquest and only wished peace at her frontiers. After the
official explanation by Austria-Hungary to Russia that it
did not claim territorial gain in Servia, the decision concerning the peace of the world rested exclusively with
St. Petersburg.

The same day the first news of Russian mobilization
reached Berlin in the evening.

The German Ambassadors at London, Paris, and
St. Petersburg were instructed to energetically point out the
danger of this Russian mobilization. The Imperial Ambassador
at St. Petersburg was also directed to make the following
declaration to the Russian Government:

see exhibit 4.

see exhibit 5.

see exhibits
6, 7, 8, 9.

see exhibits
10, 10a, 10b.

„Preparatory military measures by Russia
„will force us to counter-measures which must
„consist in mobilizing the army.

„But mobilization means war.

„As we know the obligations of France
„towards Russia, this mobilization would be directed
„against both Russia and France. We cannot
„assume that Russia desires to unchain such a
„European war. Since Austria-Hungary will not
„touch the existence of the Servian kingdom, we
„are of the opinion that Russia can afford to
„assume an attitude of waiting. We can all the
„more support the desire of Russia to protect the
„integrity of Servia as Austria-Hungary does not
„intend to question the latter. It will be easy in
„the further development of the affair to find a
„basis for an understanding."

On July 27th the Russian Secretary of War, M. Ssuchom-
linow, gave the German military attaché his word of honor
that no order to mobilize had been issued, merely preparations were being made, but not a horse mustered, nor
reserves called in. If Austria-Hungary crossed the Servian

frontier, the military districts directed towards Austria i. e. Kiev, Odessa, Moscow, Kazan, would be mobilized, under no circumstances those situated on the German frontier, i. e. St. Petersburg, Vilna, and Warsaw. Upon inquiry into the object of the mobilization against Austria-Hungary, the Russian Minister of War replied see exhibit 11. by shrugging his shoulders and referring to the diplomats. The military attaché then pointed to these mobilization measures against Austria-Hungary as extremely menacing also for Germany.

In the succeeding days news concerning Russian mobilization came at a rapid rate. Among it was also news about preparations on the German-Russian frontier, as for instance the announcement of the state of war in Kovno, the departure of the Warsaw garrison, and the strengthening of the Alexandrovo garrison.

On July 27th, the first information was received concerning preparatory measures taken by France: the 14th Corps discontinued the manoeuvres and returned to its garrison.

In the meantime we had endeavored to localize the conflict by most emphatic steps.

On July 26th, Sir Edward Grey had made the proposal to submit the differences between Austria-Hungary and Servia to a conference of the Ambassadors of Germany, France, and Italy under his chairmanship. We declared in regard to this proposal that we could not, however much we approved the idea, participate in such a conference, as we could not call Austria in her dispute with Servia before a see exhibit 12. European tribunal.

France consented to the proposal of Sir Edward Grey, but it foundered upon Austrias declining it, as was to be expected.

Faithful to our principle that mediation should not extend to the Austro-Servian conflict, which is to be considered as a purely Austro-Hungarian affair, but merely to the relations between Austria-Hungary and Russia, we continued our

endeavors to bring about an understanding be- see exhibits 13, 14.
tween these two powers.

We further declared ourselves ready, after failure of the conference idea, to transmit a second proposal of Sir Edward Grey's to Vienna in which he suggested Austria-Hungary should decide that see exhibit 15. either the Servian reply was sufficient, or that it be used as a basis for further negotiations. The Austro-Hungarian Government remarked with full appreciation of our action that it had come too late, the hostilities having already been opened. see exhibit 16.

In spite of this we continued our attempts to the utmost, and we advised Vienna to show every possible advance compatible with the dignity of the monarchy.

Unfortunately, all these proposals were overtaken by the military preparations of Russia and France.

On July 29th, the Russian Government made the official notification in Berlin that four army districts had been mobilized. At the same time further news was received concerning rapidly progressing military preparations of France, both on water and on land. see exhibit 17.

On the same day the Imperial Ambassador in St. Petersburg had an interview with the Russian Foreign Secretary, in regard to which he reported by telegraph, as follows:

> „The Secretary tried to persuade me that I should „urge my Government to participate in a quadruple „conference to find means to induce Austria-„Hungary to give up those demands which touch „upon the sovereignty of Servia. I could merely „promise to report the conversation and took the „position that, after Russia had decided upon the „baneful step of mobilization, every exchange of „ideas appeared now extremely difficult, if not „impossible. Besides, Russia now was demand-„ing from us in regard to Austria-Hungary

„the same which Austria-Hungary was being
„blamed for with regard to Servia, i. e. an
„infraction of sovereignty. Austria-Hungary
„having promised to consider the Russian
„interests by disclaiming any territorial aspiration,
„ — a great concession on the part of a state engaged
„in war — should therefore be permitted to attend
„to its affair with Servia alone. There would
„be time at the peace conference to return to
„the matter of forbearance towards the sovereignty
„of Servia.

„I added very solemnly that at this moment
„the entire Austro-Servian affair was eclipsed by
„the danger of a general European conflagration
„and I endeavored to present to the Secretary the
„magnitude of this danger.

„It was impossible to dissuade Sasonow from
„the idea that Servia could not now be deserted
„by Russia".

On July 29th, the German Military Attaché at St. Petersburg wired the following report on a conversation with the
Chief of the General Staff of the Russian army:

„The Chief of the General Staff has asked
„me to call on him, and he has told me that he
„has just come from His Majesty. He has been
„requested by the Secretary of War to reiterate
„once more that everything had remained as the
„Secretary had informed me two days ago. He
„offered confirmation in writing and gave me
„his word of honor in the most solemn manner
„that nowhere there had been a mobilization,
„viz. calling in of a single man or horse up to
„the present time, i. e. 3 o'clock in the afternoon.
„He could not assume a guaranty for the future,
„but he could emphasize that in the fronts
„directed towards our frontiers His Majesty
„desired no mobilization.

„As, however, I had received here many „pieces of news concerning the calling in of „the reserves in different parts of the country „also in Warsaw and in Vilna, I told the general „that his statements placed me before a riddle. „On his officers word of honor he replied that „such news was wrong, but that possibly here and „there a false alarm might have been given.

„I must consider this conversation as an „attempt to mislead us as to the extent of the „measures hitherto taken in view of the abundant „and positive information about the calling in of „reserves."

In reply to various inquiries concerning reasons for its threatening attitude, the Russian Government repeatedly pointed out that Austria-Hungary had commenced no conversation in St. Petersburg. The Austro-Hungarian Ambassador in St. Petersburg was therefore instructed on July 29th, at our suggestion, to enter into such conversation with Sasonow. Count Szapary was empowered to explain to the Russian minister the note to Servia though it had been overtaken by the state of war, and to accept any suggestion on the part of Russia as well as to discuss with Sasonow all questions touching directly upon the Austro-Russian relations.

Shoulder to shoulder with England we labored incessantly and supported every proposal in Vienna from which we hoped to gain the possibility of a peaceable solution of see exhibit 19. the conflict. We even as late as the 30th of July forwarded the English proposal to Vienna, as basis for negotiations, that Austria-Hungary should dictate her conditions in Servia, i. e. after her march into Servia. We thought that Russia would accept this basis.

During the interval from July 29th to July 31st there appeared renewed and cumulative news concerning Russian measures of mobilization. Accumulation of troops on the East Prussian frontier and the declaration of the state of war over all important parts of the Russian west frontier allowed no further doubt that the Russian mobilization was in full swing against us, while simultaneously all such measures were denied to our representative in St. Petersburg on word of honor.

Nay, even before the reply from Vienna regarding the Anglo-German mediation whose tendencies and basis must have been known in St. Petersburg, could possibly have been received in Berlin, Russia ordered a general mobilization.

During the same days, there took place between His Majesty the Kaiser, and Czar Nicolas an exchange of telegrams in which His Majesty called the attention of the Czar to the menacing character of the Russian mobilization during the continuance of his own mediating activities.

see exhibits 18, 20, 21, 22, 23, 23 a.

On July 31st, the Czar directed the following telegram to His Majesty the Kaiser:

„I thank You cordially for Your mediation „which permits the hope that everything may yet „end peaceably. It is technically impossible to „discontinue our military preparations which have „been made necessary by the Austrian mobilization. „It is far from us to want war. As long as the „negotiations between Austria and Servia continue, „my troops will undertake no provocative action. „I give You my solemn word thereon. I confide „with all my faith in the grace of God, and I „hope for the success of Your mediation in Vienna „for the welfare of our countries and the peace „of Europe.

Your cordially devoted
Nicolas.„

This telegram of the Czar crossed with the following sent by H. M. the Kaiser, also on July 31st, at 2 p. m.:

„Upon Your appeal to my friendship and Your „request for my aid I have engaged in mediation „between Your Government and the Government „of Austria-Hungary. While this action was „taking place, Your troops were being mobilized „against my ally Austria-Hungary, whereby, as „I have already communicated to You, my „mediation has become almost illusory. In spite „of this, I have continued it, and now I receive „reliable news that serious preparations for war „are going on on my eastern frontier. The „responsibility for the security of my country „forces me to measures of defence. I have gone „to the extreme limit of the possible in my „efforts for the preservation of the peace of the „world. It is not I who bear the responsibility „for the misfortune which now threatens the entire „civilized world. It rests in Your hand to avert „it. No one threatens the honor and peace of „Russia which might well have awaited the „success of my mediation. The friendship for „You and Your country, bequeathed to me by „my grand-father on his deathbed, has always „been sacred to me, and I have stood faithfully „by Russia while it was in serious affliction, „especially during its last war. The peace of „Europe can still be preserved by You if Russia „decides to discontinue those military prepa- „rations which menace Germany and Austria- „Hungary."

Before this telegram reached its destination, the mobilization of all the Russian forces, obviously directed against us and already ordered during the afternoon of the 31st of July, was in full swing. Notwithstanding, the telegram of the Czar was sent at 2 o'clock that same afternoon.

After the Russian general mobilization became known in Berlin, the Imperial Ambassador at St. Petersburg was instructed on the afternoon of July 31st to explain to the Russian Government that Germany declared the state of war see exhibit 24. as counter-measure against the general mobilization of the Russian army and navy which must be followed by mobilization if Russia did not cease its military measures against Germany and Austria-Hungary within 12 hours, and notified Germany thereof.

At the same time the Imperial Ambassador in Paris was instructed to demand from the French Government a declaration within 18 hours, whether it would remain neutral see exhibit 25. in a Russo-German war.

The Russian Government destroyed through its mobilization, menacing the security of our country, the laborious action at mediation of the European cabinets. The Russian mobilization in regard to the seriousness of which the Russian Government was never allowed by us to entertain a doubt, in connection with its continued denial, shows clearly that Russia wanted war.

The Imperial Ambassador at St. Petersburg delivered his note to M. Sasonow on July 31st at 12 o'clock midnight.

The reply of the Russian Government has never reached us.

Two hours after the expiration of the time limit the Czar telegraphed to H. M. the Kaiser, as follows:

> „I have received Your telegram. I comprehend „that You are forced to mobilize, but I should „like to have from You the same guaranty which „I have given You, viz., that these measures do „not mean war, and that we shall continue to „negotiate for the welfare of our two countries „and the universal peace which is so dear to our „hearts. With the aid of God it must be possible „to our long tried friendship to prevent the „shedding of blood. I expect with full confidence „Your urgent reply."

To this H. M. the Kaiser replied:

> „I thank You for Your telegram. I have
> „shown yesterday to Your Government the way
> „through which alone war may yet be averted.
> „Although I asked for a reply by to-day noon,
> „no telegram from my Ambassador has reached
> „me with the reply of Your Government.
> „I therefore have been forced to mobilize my
> „army. An immediate, clear and unmistakable
> „reply of Your Government is the sole way to
> „avoid endless misery. Until I receive this reply
> „I am unable, to my great grief, to enter upon
> „the subject of Your telegram. I must ask most
> „earnestly that You, without delay, order Your
> „troops to commit, under no circumstances, the
> „slightest violation of our frontiers."

As the time limit given to Russia had expired without the receipt of a reply to our inquiry, H. M. the Kaiser ordered the mobilization of the entire German Army and Navy on August 1st at 5 p. m.

The German Ambassador at St. Petersburg was instructed that, in the event of the Russian Government not giving a satisfactory reply within the stipulated time, he should declare that we considered ourselves in a state of war after the refusal of our demands. However, before a confirmation of the execution of this order had been received, that is to say, already in the afternoon of August 1st, i. e., the same afternoon on which the telegram of the Czar, cited above, was sent, Russian troops crossed our frontier and marched into German territory. see exhibit 26.

Thus Russia began the war against us.

Meanwhile the Imperial Ambassador in Paris put our question to the French Cabinet on July 31st at 7 p. m.

The French Prime Minister gave an equivocal and unsatisfactory reply on August 1st at 1. p. m. which gave no see exhibit 27. clear idea of the position of France, as he limited himself to the explanation that France would do that which her interests demanded. A few hours later, at 5 p. m., the mobilization of the entire French army and navy was ordered.

On the morning of the next day France opened hostilities.

THE ORIGINAL

TELEGRAMS

AND

NOTES.

The Note of Austria-Hungary to Servia,
Presented July 23rd in Belgrade.

„On March 31st, 1909, the Royal Servian Minister to the Court of Vienna made the following statement, by order of his Government:

„Servia declares that she is not affected in „her rights by the situation established in Bosnia, „and that she will therefore adapt herself to the „decisions which the powers are going to arrive at „in reference to Art. 25 of the Berlin Treaty. By „following the councils of the powers, Servia „binds herself to cease the attitude of protest „and resistence which she has assumed since last „October, relative to the annexation, and she „binds herself further to change the direction of „her present policies towards Austria-Hungary, „and, in the future, to live with the latter in „friendly and neighborly relations.

„The history of the last years, and especially the painful events of June 28th, have demonstrated the existence of a subversive movement in Servia whose aim it is to separate certain territories from the Austro-Hungarian monarchy. This movement, which developed under the eyes of the Servian Government, has found expression subsequently beyond the territory of the kingdom, in acts of terrorism, a series of assassinations and murders.

„Far from fulfilling the formal obligations contained in the declaration of March 31st, 1909, the Royal Servian Government has done nothing to suppress this movement.

She suffered the criminal doings of the various societies and associations directed against the monarchy, the unbridled language of the press, the glorification of the originators of assassinations, the participation of officers and officials in subversive intrigues; she suffered the unwholesome propaganda in public education, and lastly permitted all manifestations which would mislead the Servian people into hatred of the monarchy and into contempt for its institutions.

„This sufferance of which the Royal Servian Government made itself guilty, has lasted up to the moment in which the events of June 28th demonstrated to the entire world the ghastly consequences of such sufferance.

„It becomes plain from the evidence and confessions of the criminal authors of the outrage of June 28th, that the murder at Sarajevo was conceived in Belgrade, that the murderers received the arms and bombs with which they were equipped, from Servian officers and officials who belonged to the Narodna Odbrana, and that, lastly, the transportation of the criminals and their arms to Bosnia was arranged and carried out by leading Servian frontier officials.

„The cited results of the investigation do not permit the Imperial and Royal Government to observe any longer the attitude of waiting, which it has assumed for years towards those agitations which have their centre in Belgrade, and which from there radiate into the territory of the monarchy. These results, on the contrary, impose upon the Imperial and Royal Government the duty to terminate intrigues which constitute a permanent menace for the peace of the monarchy.

„In order to obtain this purpose, the Imperial and Royal Government is forced to demand official assurance from the Servian Government that it condemns the propaganda directed against Austria-Hungary, i. e. the entirety of the machinations whose aim it is to separate parts from the monarchy which belong to it, and that she binds herself to suppress with all means this criminal and terrorizing propaganda.

„In order to give to these obligations a solemn character, the Royal Servian Government will publish on the first page of its official organ of July 26th, 1914, the following declaration:

> „The Royal Servian Government condemns „the propaganda directed against Austria-Hungary, „i. e. the entirety of those machinations whose „aim it is to separate from the Austro-Hungarian „monarchy territories belonging thereto, and she „regrets sincerely the ghastly consequences of „these criminal actions.

> „The Royal Servian Government regrets that „Servian officers and officials have participated „in the propaganda, cited above, and have thus „threatened the friendly and neighborly relations „which the Royal Government was solemnly „bound to cultivate by its declaration of March „31st, 1909.

> „The Royal Government which disapproves „and rejects every thought or every attempt at „influencing the destinations of the inhabitants „of any part of Austria-Hungary, considers it its „duty to call most emphatically to the attention „of its officers and officials, and of the entire „population of the kingdom, that it will hence-„forward proceed with the utmost severity against „any persons guilty of similar actions, to prevent „and suppress which it will make every effort."

„This explanation is to be brought simultaneously to the cognizance of the Royal Army through an order of H. M. the King, and it is to be published in the official organ of the Army.

„The Royal Servian Government binds itself, in addition, as follows:

1. to suppress any publication which fosters hatred of, and contempt for, the Austro-Hungarian monarchy, and whose general tendency is directed against the latters territorial integrity;

2. to proceed at once with the dissolution of the society Narodna Odbrana, to confiscate their entire means of propaganda, and to proceed in the same manner against the other societies and associations in Servia which occupy themselves with the propaganda against Austria-Hungary. The Royal Government will take the necessary measures, so that the dissolved societies may not continue their activities under another name or in another form;

3. without delay to eliminate from the public instruction in Servia, so far as the corps of instructors, as well as the means of instruction are concerned, that which serves, or may serve, to foster the propaganda against Austria-Hungary;

4. to remove from military service and the administration in general all officers and officials who are guilty of propaganda against Austria-Hungary, and whose names, with a communication of the material which the Imperial and Royal Government possesses against them, the Imperial and Royal Government reserves the right to communicate to the Royal Government;

5. to consent that in Servia officials of the Imperial and Royal Government co-operate in the suppression of a movement directed against the territorial integrity of the monarchy;

6. to commence a judicial investigation against the participants of the conspiracy of June 28th, who are on Servian territory. Officials, delegated by the Imperial and Royal Government will participate in the examinations;

7. to proceed at once with all severity to arrest Major Voja Tankosic and a certain Milan Ciganowic, Servian State officials, who have been compromised through the result of the investigation;

8. to prevent through effective measures the participation of the Servian authorities in the smuggling of arms and explosives across the frontier and to dismiss those officials of Shabatz and Loznica, who assisted the originators of the crime of Sarajevo in crossing the frontier;

9. to give to the Imperial and Royal Government explanations in regard to the unjustifiable remarks of high Servian functionaries in Servia and abroad who have not hesitated, in spite of their official position, to express themselves in interviews in a hostile manner against Austria-Hungary after the outrage of June 28th.

10. The Imperial and Royal Government expects a reply from the Royal Government at the latest until Saturday 25th inst., at 6 p. m. A memoir concerning the results of the investigations at Sarajevo, so far as they concern points 7. and 8. is enclosed with this note."

Enclosure.

The investigation carried on against Gabrilo Princip and accomplices in the Court of Sarajevo, on account of the assassination on June 28th has, so far, yielded the following results:

1. The plan to murder Arch-Duke Franz Ferdinand during his stay in Sarajevo was conceived in Belgrade by Gabrilo Princip, Nedeljko, Gabrinowic, and a certain Milan Ciganowic and Trifko Grabez, with the aid of Major Voja Tankosic.

2. The six bombs and four Browning pistols which were used by the criminals, were obtained by Milan Ciganowic and Major Tankosic, and presented to Princip Gabrinowic in Belgrade.

3. The bombs are hand grenades, manufactured at the arsenal of the Servian Army in Kragujevac.

4. To insure the success of the assassination, Milan Ciganowic instructed Princip Gabrinowic in the use of the grenades and gave instructions in shooting with Browning pistols to Princip Grabez in a forest near the targed practice field of Topshider — (outside Belgrade). —

5. In order to enable the crossing of the frontier of Bosnia and Herzegovina by Princip Gabrinowic and Grabez, and the smuggling of their arms, a secret system of transportation was organized by Ciganowic. The entry of the criminals with their arms into Bosnia and Herzegovina was effected by the frontier captains of Shabatz (Rade Popowic) and of Loznica, as well as by the custom house official Rudivoy Grbic of Loznica with the aid of several other persons.

The Servian Answer.

Presented at Vienna, July 25 th, 1914.

(With Austria's commentaries [in italics].)

The Royal Government has received the communication of the Imperial and Royal Government of the 23 rd inst. and is convinced that its reply will dissipate any misunderstanding which threatens to destroy the friendly and neighborly relations between the Austrian monarchy and the kingdom of Servia.

The Royal Government is conscious that nowhere there have been renewed protests against the great neighborly monarchy like those which at one time were expressed in the Skuptschina, as well as in the declaration and actions of the responsible representatives of the state at that time, and which were terminated by the Servian declaration of March 31st 1909; furthermore that since that time neither the different corporations of the kingdom, nor the officials have made an attempt to alter the political and judicial condition created in Bosnia and the Herzegovina. The

Royal Government states that the I. and R. Government has made no protestation in this sense excepting in the case of a text book, in regard to which the I. und R. Government has received an entirely satisfactory explanation. Servia has given during the time of the Balcan crisis in numerous cases evidence of her pacific and moderate policy, and it is only owing to Servia and the sacrifices which she has brought in the interest of the peace of Europe that this peace has been preserved.

The Royal Servian Government limits itself to establishing that since the declaration of March 31st 1909, there has been no attempt on the part of the Servian Government to alter the position of Bosnia and the Herzegovina.

With this she deliberately shifts the foundation of our note, as we have not insisted that she and her officials have undertaken anything official in this direction. Our gravamen is that in spite of the obligation assumed in the cited note, she has omitted to suppress the movement directed against the territorial integrity of the monarchy.

Her obligation consisted in changing her attitude and the entire direction of her policies, and in entering into friendly and neighborly relations with the Austro-Hungarian monarchy, and not only not to interfere with the possession of Bosnia.

The Royal Government cannot be made responsible for expressions of a private character, as for instance newspaper articles and the peaceable work of societies, expressions which are of very common appearance in other countries, and which ordinarily are not under the control of the state. This, all the less, as the Royal Government has shown great courtesy in the solution of a whole series of questions which have arisen between Servia and Austria-Hungary, whereby it has succeeded to solve the greater number thereof, in favor of the progress of both countries.

The assertion of the Royal Servian Government that the expressions of the press and the activity of Servian associations possess a private character and thus escape governmental control, stands in full contrast with the institutions of modern states and even the most liberal of press and society laws, which nearly everywhere subject the press and the societies to a certain control of the state. This is also provided for by the Servian institutions. The rebuke against the Servian Government consists in the fact that it has totally omitted to supervise its press and its societies, in so far as it knew their direction to be hostile to the monarchy.

The Royal Government was therefore painfully surprised by the assertions that citizens of Servia had participated in the preparations of the outrage in Sarajevo. The Government expected to be invited to cooperate in the investigation of the crime, and it was ready in order to prove its complete correctness, to proceed against all persons in regard to whom it would receive information.

This assertion is incorrect. The Servian Government was accurately informed about the suspicion resting upon quite definite personalities and not only in the position, but also obliged by its own laws to institute investigations spontaneously. The Servian Government has done nothing in this direction.

According to the wishes of the I. and R. Government, the Royal Government is prepared to surrender to the court, without regard to position and rank, every Servian citizen, for whose participation in the crime of Sarajevo it should have received proof. It binds itself particularly on the first page of the official organ of the 26th of July to publish the following enunciation:

> „The Royal Servian Government condemns „every propaganda which should be directed „against Austria-Hungary, i. e. the entirety of „such activities as aim towards the separation of „certain territories from the Austro-Hungarian „monarchy, and it regrets sincerely the lamentable „consequences of these criminal machinations.“

The Austrian demand reads:

> ,,The Royal Servian Government condemns the „propaganda against Austria-Hungary . . . . . .“

*The alteration of the declaration as demanded by us, which
has been made by the Royal Servian Government, is meant
to imply that a propaganda directed against Austria-Hungary
does not exist, and that it is not aware of such. This
formula is insincere, and the Servian Government reserves
itself the supterfuge for later occasions that it had not disavowed
by this declaration the existing propaganda, nor recognized
the same as hostile to the monarchy, whence it could deduce
further that it is not obliged to suppress in the future a
propaganda similar to the present one.*

The Royal Government regrets that according to a
communication of the I. and R. Government certain Servian
officers and functionaries have participated in the propaganda
just referred to, and that these have therefore endangered
the amicable relations for the observation of which the Royal
Government had solemnly obliged itself through the
declaration of March 31st, 1909.

The Government . . . identical with the demanded text.

The formula as demanded by Austria reads:

> *„The Royal Government regrets that Servian
> „officers and functionaries . . . . have parti-
> „cipated . . . . „*

*Also with this formula and the further addition „according
to the declaration of the I. and R. Government“, the Servian
Government pursues the object, already indicated above, to
preserve a free hand for the future.*

The Royal Government binds itself further:

1. During the next regular meeting of the Skuptschina
to embody in the press laws a clause, to wit, that the
incitement to hatred of, and contempt for, the monarchy is
to be must severely punished, as well as every publication
whose general tendency is directed against the territorial
integrity of Austria-Hungary.

It binds itself in view of the coming revision of the
constitution to embody an amendment into Art. 22 of the
constitutional law which permits the confiscation of such

publications as is at present impossible according to the clear definition of Art. 22 of the constitution.

Austria had demanded:

1. ＞*To suppress every publication which incites to hatred and contempt for the monarchy, and whose tendency is directed against the territorial integrity of the monarchy.*《

   We wanted to bring about the obligation for Servia to take care that such attacks of the press would cease in the future.

   Instead Servia offers to pass certain laws which are meant as means towards this end, viz.:

   a) *A law according to which the expressions of the press hostile to the monarchy can be individually punished, a matter, which is immaterial to us, all the more so, as the individual prosecution of press intrigues is very rarely possible and as, with a lax enforcement of such laws, the few cases of this nature would not be punished. The proposition, therefore, does not meet our demand in any way, and it offers not the least guarantee for the desired success.*

   b) *An amendment to Art. 22 of the constitution, which would permit confiscation, a proposal, which does not satisfy us, as the existence of such a law in Servia is of no use to us. For we want the obligation of the Government to enforce it and that has not been promised us.*

These proposals are therefore entirely unsatisfactory and evasive as we are not told within what time these laws will be passed, and as in the event of the notpassing of these laws by the Skuptschina everything would remain as it is, excepting the event of a possible resignation of the Government.

2. The Government possesses no proofs and the note of the I. and R. Government does not submit them that the society Narodna Odbrana and other similar societies have committed, up to the present, any criminal actions of this manner through anyone of their members. Notwithstanding

this, the Royal Government will accept the demand of the I. and R. Government and dissolve the society Narodna Odbrana, as well as every society which should act against Austria-Hungary.

The propaganda of the Narodna Odbrana and affiliated societies hostile to the monarchy fills the entire public life of Servia; it is therefore an entirely inacceptable reserve if the Servian Government asserts that it knows nothing about it. Aside from this, our demand is not completely fulfilled, as we have asked besides:

> *,,To confiscate the means of propaganda of ,,these societies to prevent the reformation of the ,,dissolved societies under another name and in ,,another form."*

In these two directions the Belgrade Cabinet is perfectly silent, so that through this semi-concession there is offered us no guarantee for putting an end to the agitation of the associations hostile to the Monarchy, especially the Narodna Odbrana.

3. The Royal Servian Government binds itself without delay to eliminate from the public instruction in Servia anything which might further the propaganda directed against Austria-Hungary provided the I. and R. Government furnishes actual proofs.

Also in this case the Servian Government first demands proofs for a propaganda hostile to the Monarchy in the public instruction of Servia while it must know that the text books introduced in the Servian schools contain objectionable matter in this direction and that a large portion of the teachers are in the camp of the Narodna Odbrana and affiliated societies.

Furthermore, the Servian Government has not fulfilled a part of our demands, as we have requested, as it omitted in its text the addition desired by us: ,,as far as the body of instructors is concerned, as well as the means of instruction" — a sentence which shows clearly where the propaganda hostile to the Monarchy is to be found in the Servian schools.

4. The Royal Government is also ready to dismiss those officers and officials from the military and civil services in regard to whom it has been proved by judicial investigation that they have been guilty of actions against the territorial integrity of the monarchy; it expects that the I. and R. Government communicate to it for the purpose of starting the investigation the names of these officers and officials, and the facts with which they have been charged.

By promising the dismissal from the military and civil services of those officers and officials who are found guilty by judicial procedure, the Servian Government limits its assent to those cases, in which these persons have been charged with a crime according to the statutory code. As, however, we demand the removal of such officers and officials as indulge in a propaganda hostile to the Monarchy, which is generally not punishable in Servia, our demands have not been fulfilled in this point.

5. The Royal Government confesses that it is not clear about the sense and the scope of that demand of the I. and R. Government which concerns the obligation on the part of the Royal Servian Government to permit the cooperation of officials of the I. and R. Government on Servian territory, but it declares that it is willing to accept every cooperation which does not run counter to international law and criminal law, as well as to the friendly and neighborly relations.

The international law, as well as the criminal law, has nothing to do with this question; it is purely a matter of the nature of state police which is to be solved by way of a special agreement. The reserved attitude of Servia is therefore incomprehensible and on account of its vague general form it would lead to unbridgeable difficulties.

6. The Royal Government considers it its duty as a matter of course to begin an investigation against all those persons who have participated in the outrage of June 28th and who are in its territory. As far as the cooperation in this investigation of specially delegated officials of the I. and R. Government is concerned, this cannot be accepted, as

this is a violation of the constitution and of criminal procedure. Yet in some cases the result of the investigation might be communicated to the Austro-Hungarian officials.

The Austrian demand was clear and unmistakable:

1. *To institute a criminal procedure against the participants in the outrage.*
2. *Participation by I. and R. Government officials in the examinations (,,Recherche" in contrast with ,,enquête judiciaire").*
3. *It did not occur to us to let I. and R. Government officials participate in the Servian court procedure; they were to cooperate only in the police researches which had to furnish and fix the material for the investigation.*

If the Servian Government misunderstands us here, this is done deliberately, for it must be familiar with the difference between ,,enquête judiciaire" and simple police researches. As it desired to escape from every control of the investigation which would yield, if correctly carried out, highly undesirable results for it, and as it possesses no means to refuse in a plausible manner the cooperation of our officials (precedents for such police intervention exist in great number) it tries to justify its refusal by showing up our demands as impossible.

7. The Royal Government has ordered on the evening of the day on which the note was received the arrest of Major Voislar Tankosic. However, as far as Milan Ciganowic is concerned who is a citizen of the Austro-Hungarian Monarchy and who has been employed till June 28th with the Railroad Department, it has as yet been impossible to locate him, wherefor a warrant has been issued against him.

The I. and R. Government is asked to make known, as soon as possible, for the purpose of conducting the investigation, the existing grounds for suspicion and the proofs of guilt, obtained in the investigation at Sarajevo.

This reply is disingenuous. According to our investigation, Ciganowic, by order of the police prefect in Belgrade, left three days after the outrage for Ribari, after it had become known that Ciganowic had participated in the outrage. In the first place, it is therefore incorrect that Ciganowic left the Servian service on June 28th. In the second place, we add that the prefect of police at Belgrade who had himself caused the departure of this Ciganowic and who knew his whereabouts, declared in an interview that a man by the name of Milan Ciganowic did not exist in Belgrade.

8. The Servian Government will amplify and render more severe the existing measures against the suppression of smuggling of arms and explosives.

It is a matter of course that it will proceed at once against, and punish severely, those officials of the frontier service on the line Shabatz-Loznica who violated their duty and who have permitted the perpetrators of the crime to cross the frontier.

9. The Royal Government is ready to give explanations about the expressions which its officials in Servia and abroad have made in interviews after the outrage and which, according to the assertion of the I. and R. Government, were hostile to the Monarchy. As soon as the I. and R. Government points out in detail where those expressions were made and succeeds in proving that those expressions have actually been made by the functionaries concerned, the Royal Government itself will take care that the necessary evidences and proofs are collected therefor.

The Royal Servian Government must be aware of the interviews in question. If it demands of the I. and R. Government that it should furnish all kinds of detail about the said interviews and if it reserves for itself the right of a formal investigation, it shows that it is not its intention seriously to fulfill the demand.

10. The Royal Government will notify the I. and R. Government, so far as this has not been already done by the present note, of the execution of the measures in question as soon as one of those measures has been ordered and put into execution.

The Royal Servian Government believes it to be to the common interest not to rush the solution of this affair and it is therefore, in case the I. and R. Government should not consider itself satisfied with this answer, ready, as ever, to accept a peaceable solution, be it by referring the decision of this question to the International Court at the Hague or by leaving it to the decision of the Great Powers who have participated in the working out of the declaration given by the Servian Government on March 31st 1909."

The Servian Note, therefore, is entirely a play for time.

Exhibit 1.

The Chancellor to the Imperial Ambassadors at Paris, London, and St. Petersburg, on Juli 23rd 1914.

The publications of the Austro-Hungarian Government concerning the circumstances under which the assassination of the Austrian successor to the throne and his consort took place, disclose clearly the aims which the pan-Serb propaganda has set itself and the means which it utilizes for their realization. Through the published facts the last doubt must disappear that the center of action of the efforts for the separation of the south slavic provinces from the Austro-Hungarian Monarchy and their union with the Servian Kingdom must be sought in Belgrade where it displays its activity with the connivance of members of the Government and of the Army.

The Serb intrigues may be traced back through a series of years. In a specially marked manner the pan-Serb chauvinism showed itself during the Bosnian crisis. Only to the far-reaching self-restraint and moderation of the Austro-Hungarian Government and the energetic intercession of the powers is it to be ascribed that the provocations to which at that time Austria-Hungary was exposed on the part of Servia, did not lead to a conflict. The assurance of future well-behaviour which the Servian Government gave at that time, it has not kept. Under the very eyes, at least with the tacit sufferance of official Servia, the pan-Serb propaganda has meanwhile increased in scope and intensity; at its door is to be laid the latest crime the threads of which lead to Belgrade. It has become evident that it is compatible neither with the dignity nor with the self-preservation of the Austro-Hungarian Monarchy to view any longer idly the doings across the border through which the safety and the integrity of the

Monarchy are permanently threatened. With this state of affairs, the action as well as the demands of the Austro-Hungarian government can be viewed only as justifiable. Nevertheless, the attitude assumed by public opinion as well as by the government in Servia does not preclude the fear that the Servian government will decline to meet these demands and that it will allow itself to be carried away into a provocative attitude toward Austria-Hungary. Nothing would remain for the Austro-Hungarian government, unless it renounced definitely its position as a great power, but to press its demands with the Servian government and, if need be, enforce the same by appeal to military measures, in regard to which the choice of means must be left with it.

I have the honor to request you to express yourself in the sense indicated above to (the present representative of M. Viviani) (Sir Edward Grey) (M. Sasonow) and therewith give special emphasis to the view that in this question there is concerned an affair which should be settled solely between Austria-Hungary and Servia, the limitation to which it must be the earnest endeavor of the powers to insure. We anxiously desire the localisation of the conflict because every intercession of another power on account of the various treaty-alliances would precipitate inconceivable consequences.

I shall look forward with interest to a telegraphic report about the course of your interview.

Exhibit 2.

The Chancellor to the Governments of Germany.
Confidential. Berlin, July 28 th, 1914.

You will make the following report to the Government to which you are accredited:

In view of the facts which the Austrian Government has published in its note to the Servian Government, the last doubt must disappear that the outrage to which the Austro-Hungarian successor to the throne has fallen a victim, was prepared in Servia, to say the least with the connivance of members of the Servian government and army. It is a product of the pan-Serb intrigues which for a series of years have become a source of permanent disturbance for the Austro-Hungarian Monarchy and for the whole of Europe.

The pan-Serb chauvinism appeared especially marked during the Bosnian crisis. Only to the far-reaching self-restraint and moderation of the Austro-Hungarian government and the energetic intercession of the powers is it to be ascribed that the provocations to which Austria-Hungary was exposed at that time, did not lead to a conflict. The assurance of future well-behaviour, which the Servian government gave at that time, it has not kept. Under the very eyes, at least with the tacit sufferance of official Servia, the pan-Serb propaganda has meanwhile continued to increase in scope and intensity. It would be compatible neither with its dignity nor with its right to self-preservation if the Austro-Hungarian government persisted to view idly any longer the intrigues beyond the frontier, through which the safety and the integrity of the monarchy are permanently threatened. With this state of affairs, the action as well as the demands of the Austro-Hungarian Government can be viewed only as justifiable.

The reply of the Servian government to the demands which the Austro-Hungarian government put on the 23rd inst. through its representative in Belgrade, shows that the dominating factors in Servia are not inclined to cease their former policies and agitation. There will remain nothing else for the Austro-Hungarian government than to press its demands, if need be through military action, unless it renounces for good its position as a great power.

Some Russian personalities deem it their right as a matter of course and a task of Russia's to actively become a party to Servia in the conflict between Austria-Hungary and Servia. For the European conflagration which would result from a similar step by Russia, the «Nowoje Wremja» believes itself justified in making Germany responsible in so far as it does not induce Austria-Hungary to yield.

The Russian press thus turns conditions upside down. It is not Austria-Hungary which has called forth the conflict with Servia, but it is Servia which, through unscrupulous favor toward pan-Serb aspirations, even in parts of the Austro-Hungarian monarchy, threatens the same in her existence and creates conditions, which eventually found expression in the wanton outrage at Sarajevo. If Russia believes that it must champion the cause of Servia in this matter, it certainly has the right to do so. However, it must realize that it makes the Serb activities its own, to undermine the conditions of existence of the Austro-Hungarian monarchy, and that thus it bears the sole responsibility if out of the Austro-Servian affair, which all other great powers desire to localize, there arises a European war. This responsibility of Russia's is evident and it weighs the more heavily as Count Berchtold has officially declared to Russia that Austria-Hungary has no intention to acquire Servian territory or to touch the existence of the Servian Kingdom, but only desires peace against the Servian intrigues threatening its existence.

The attitude of the Imperial government in this question is clearly indicated. The agitation conducted by the pan-Slavs in Austria-Hungary has for its goal, with the destruction of the Austro-Hungarian monarchy, the scattering or weakening of the triple alliance with a complete isolation of the German Empire in consequence. Our own interest therefore calls us to the side of Austria-Hungary. The duty, if at all possible, to guard Europe against a universal war, points to the support by ourselves of those endeavors which aim at the localization of the conflict, faithful to the course of those policies which we have carried out successfully for forty-four years in the interest of the preservation of the peace of Europe.

Should, however, against our hope, through the interference of Russia the fire be spread, we should have to support, faithful to our duty as allies, the neighbor-monarchy with all the power at our command. We shall take the sword only if forced to it, but then in the clear consciousness that we are not guilty of the calamity which war will bring upon the peoples of Europe.

Exhibit 3.

Telegram of the Imperial Ambassador at Vienna to the Chancellor on July 24th 1914.

Count Berchtold has asked to-day for the Russian Chargé d'affaires in order to explain to him thoroughly and cordially Austria-Hungary's point of view toward Servia. After recapitulation of the historical development of the past few years, he emphasized that the Monarchy entertained no thought of conquest toward Servia. Austria-Hungary would not claim Servian territory. It insisted merely that this step was meant as a definite means of checking the Serb intrigues. Impelled by force of circumstance, Austria-Hungary must have a guaranty for continued amicable relations with Servia. It was far from him to intend to bring about a change in the balance of powers in the Balcan. The Chargé d'affaires who had received no instructions from St. Petersburg, took the discussion of the Secretary „ad referendum" with the promise to submit it immediately to Sasonow.

Exhibit 4.

Telegram of the Imperial Ambassador at St. Petersburg to the Chancellor on July 24th 1914.

I have just utilized the contents of Order 592 in a prolonged interview with Sasonow. The Secretary (Sasonow) indulged in unmeasured accusations toward Austria-Hungary and he was very much agitated. He declared most positively that Russia could not permit under any circumstances that the Servo-Austrian difficulty be settled alone between the parties concerned.

Exhibit 5.

The Imperial Ambassador at St. Petersburg to the Chancellor.
Telegram of July 26th 1914.

The Austro-Hungarian Ambassador had an extended interview with Sasonow this afternoon. Both parties had a satisfactory impression as they told me afterwards. The assurance of the Ambassador that Austria-Hungary had no idea of conquest but wished to obtain peace at last at her frontiers, greatly pacified the Secretary.

Exhibit 6.

Telegram of the Imperial Ambassador at St. Petersburg
to the Chancellor on July 25th 1914.

Message to H. M. from General von Chelius (German honorary aide de camp to the Czar).

The manoeuvres of the troops in the Krasnoe camp were suddenly interrupted and the regiments returned to their garrisons at once. The manoeuvres have been cancelled. The military pupils were raised to-day to the rank of officers instead of next fall. At headquarters there obtains great excitement over the procedure of Austria. I have the impression that complete preparations for mobilization against Austria are being made.

Exhibit 7.

Telegram of the Imperial Ambassador at St. Petersburg
to the Chancellor on July 26th 1914.

The military attaché requests the following message to be sent to the general staff:

I deem it certain that mobilisation has been ordered for Kiev and Odessa. It is doubtful at Warsaw and Moscow and improbable elsewhere.

Exhibit 8.

Telegram of the Imperial Consulate at Kovno to the
Chancellor on July 27th 1914.

Kovno has been declared to be in a state of war.

Exhibit 9.

Telegram of the Imperial Minister at Berne to the Chancellor on July 27th 1914.

Have learned reliably that French XIVth corps has discontinued manoeuvres.

Exhibit 10.

Telegram of the Chancellor to the Imperial Ambassador at London. Urgent. July 26th 1914.

Austria-Hungary has declared in St. Petersburg officially and solemnly that it has no desire for territorial gain in Servia; that it will not touch the existence of the Kingdom, but that it desires to establish peaceful conditions. According to news received here, the call for several classes of the reserves is expected immediately which is equivalent to mobilization. If this news proves correct, we shall be forced to contermeasures very much against our own wishes. Our desire to localize the conflict and to preserve the peace of Europe remains unchanged. We ask to act in this sense at St. Petersburg with all possible emphasis.

Exhibit 10a.

Telegram of the Imperial Chancellor to the Imperial Ambassador at Paris. July 26th 1914.

After officially declaring to Russia that Austria-Hungary has no intention to acquire territorial gain and to touch the existence of the Kingdom, the decision whether there is to be a European war rests solely with Russia which has to bear the entire responsibility. We depend upon France with which we are at one in the desire for the preservation of the peace of Europe that it will exercise its influence at St. Petersburg in favour of peace.

Exhibit 10b.

Telegram of the Chancellor to the Imperial Ambassador at St. Petersburg on July 26th 1914.

After Austria's solemn declaration of its territorial disinterestedness, the responsibility for a possible disturbance of the peace of Europe through a Russian intervention rests solely upon Russia. We trust still that Russia will undertake no steps which will threaten seriously the peace of Europe.

Exhibit 11.

Telegram of the Imperial Ambassador at St. Petersburg to the Chancellor on July 27th 1914.

Military Attaché reports a conversation with the Secretary of War:

Sasonow has requested the latter to enlighten me on the situation. The Secretary of War has given me his word of honor that no order to mobilize has as yet been issued. Though general preparations are being made, no reserves were called and no horses mustered. If Austria crossed the Servian frontier, such military districts as are directed toward Austria, viz., Kiev, Odessa, Moscow, Kazan, are to be mobilized. Under no circumstances those on the German frontier, Warsaw, Vilna, St. Petersburg. Peace with Germany was desired very much. Upon my inquiry into the object of mobilization against Austria he shrugged his shoulders and referred to the diplomats. I told the Secretary that we appreciated the friendly intentions, but considered mobilization even against Austria as very menacing.

Exhibit 12.

Telegram of the Chancellor to the Imperial Ambassador at London on July 27th, 1914.

We know as yet nothing of a suggestion of Sir Edward Grey's to hold a quadruple conference in London. It is impossible for us to place our ally in his dispute with Servia before a European tribunal. Our mediation must be limited to the danger of an Austro-Russian conflict.

Exhibit 13.

Telegram of the Chancellor to the Imperial Ambassador at London on July 25th, 1914.

The distinction made by Sir Edward Grey between an Austro-Servian and an Austro-Russian conflict is perfectly correct. We do not wish to interpose in the former any more than England, and as heretofore we take the position that this question must be localized by virtue of all powers refraining from intervention. It is therefore our hope that Russia will refrain from any action in view of her responsibility and the seriousness of the situation. We are prepared, in the event of an Austro-Russian controversy, quite apart from our known duties as allies, to intercede between Russia and Austria jointly with the other powers.

Exhibit 14.

Telegram of the Chancellor to the Imperial Ambassador at St. Petersburg on July 28th, 1914.

We continue in our endeavor to induce Vienna to elucidate in St. Petersburg the object and scope of the Austrian action in Servia in a manner both convincing and satisfactory to Russia. The declaration of war which has meanwhile ensued alters nothing in this matter.

Exhibit 15.

Telegram of the Chancellor to the Imperial Ambassador in London on July 27th, 1914.

We have at once started the mediation proposal in Vienna in the sense as desired by Sir Edward Grey. We have communicated besides to Count Berchtold the desire of M. Sasonow for a direct parley with Vienna.

Exhibit 16.

Telegram of the Imperial Ambassador at Vienna to the Chancellor on July 28th, 1914.

Count Berchtold requests me to express to Your Excellency his thanks for the communication of the English mediation proposal. He states, however, that after the opening of hostilities by Servia and the subsequent declaration of war, the step appears belated.

Exhibit 17.

Telegram of the Chancellor to the Imperial Ambassador at Paris on July 29th, 1914.

News received here regarding French preparations of war multiplies from hour to hour. I request that You call the attention of the French Government to this and accentuate that such measures would call forth counter-measures on our part. We should have to proclaim threatening state of war (drohende Kriegsgefahr), and while this would not mean a call for the reserves or mobilization, yet the tension would be aggravated. We continue to hope for the preservation of peace.

Exhibit 18.

Telegram of the Military Attaché at St. Petersburg to H. M. the Kaiser on July 30th, 1914.

Prince Troubetzki said to me yesterday, after causing Your Majesty's telegram to be delivered at once to Czar Nicolas: Thank God that a telegram of Your Emperor has come. He has just told me the telegram has made a deep impression upon the Czar but as the mobilization against

Austria had already been ordered and Sasonow had convinced His Majesty that it was no longer possible to retreat, His Majesty was sorry he could not change it any more. I then told him that the guilt for the measureless consequences lay at the door of premature mobilization against Austria-Hungary which after all was involved merely in a local war with Servia, for Germany's answer was clear and the responsibility rested upon Russia which ignored Austria-Hungary's assurance that it had no intentions of territorial gain in Servia. Austria-Hungary mobilized against Servia and not against Russia and there was no ground for an immediate action on the part of Russia. I further added that in Germany one could not understand any more Russia's phrase that „she could not desert her brethren in Servia", after the horrible crime of Sarajevo. I told him finally he need not wonder if Germany's army were to be mobilized.

Exhibit 19.

Telegram of the Chancellor to the Imperial Ambassador at Rome on July 31ˢᵗ, 1914.

We have continued to negotiate between Russia and Austria-Hungary through a direct exchange of telegrams between His Majesty the Kaiser and His Majesty the Czar, as well as in conjunction with Sir Edward Grey. Through the mobilization of Russia all our efforts have been greatly handicapped if they have not become impossible. In spite of pacifying assurances Russia is taking such far-reaching measures against us that the situation is becoming continually more menacing.

Exhibit 20.

I. His Majesty to the Czar.

July 28ᵗʰ, 10.45 p. m.

I have heard with the greatest anxiety of the impression which is caused by the action of Austria-Hungary against

Servia. The inscrupulous agitation which has been going on for years in Servia, has led to the revolting crime of which Archduke Franz Ferdinand has become a victim. The spirit which made the Servians murder their own King and his consort, still dominates that country. Doubtless You will agree with me that both of us, You as well as I, and all other sovereigns, have a common interest to insist that all those who are responsible for this horrible murder, shall suffer their deserved punishment.

On the other hand I by no means overlook the difficulty encountered by You and Your Government to stem the tide of public opinion. In view of the cordial friendship which has joined us both for a long time with firm ties, I shall use my entire influence to induce Austria-Hungary to obtain a frank and satisfactory understanding with Russia. I hope confidently that You will support me in my efforts to overcome all difficulties which may yet arise.

Your most sincere and devoted friend and cousin

signed: Wilhelm.

Exhibit 21.

II. The Czar to His Majesty.

Peterhof Palace, July 29 th, 1 p. m.

I am glad that You are back in Germany. In this serious moment I ask You earnestly to help me. An ignominious war has been declared against a weak country and in Russia the indignation which I fully share is tremendous. I fear that very soon I shall be unable to resist the pressure exercised upon me and that I shall be forced to take measures which will lead to war. To prevent a calamity as a European war would be, I urge You in the name of our old friendship to do all in Your power to restrain Your ally from going too far.

signed: Nicolas.

Exhibit 22.

III. His Majesty to the Czar.

July 29th, 6.30 p. m.

I have received Your telegram and I share Your desire for the conservation of peace. However: I cannot — as I told You in my first telegram — consider the action of Austria-Hungary as an „ignominious war". Austria-Hungary knows from experience that the promises of Servia as long as they are merely on paper are entirely unreliable.

According to my opinion the action of Austria-Hungary is to be considered as an attempt to receive full guaranty that the promises of Servia are effectively translated into deeds. In this opinion I am strengthened by the explanation of the Austrian cabinet that Austria-Hungary intended no territorial gain at the expense of Servia. I am therefore of opinion that it is perfectly possible for Russia to remain a spectator in the Austro-Servian war without drawing Europe into the most terrible war it has ever seen. I believe that a direct understanding is possible and desirable between Your Government and Vienna, an understanding which — as I have already telegraphed You — my Government endeavors to aid with all possible effort. Naturally military measures by Russia, which might be construed as a menace by Austria-Hungary, would accelerate a calamity which both of us desire to avoid and would undermine my position as mediator which — upon Your appeal to my friendship and aid — I willingly accepted.

signed: Wilhelm.

Exhibit 23.

IV. His Majesty to the Czar.

July 30th, 1 a. m.

My Ambassador has instructions to direct the attention of Your Government to the dangers and serious consequences of a mobilization; I have told You the same in my last telegram. Austria-Hungary has mobilized only against Servia, and only a part of her army. If Russia, as seems to be the case according to Your advice and that of Your Government, mobilizes against Austria-Hungary, the part of the mediator with which You have entrusted me in such friendly manner and which I have accepted upon Your express desire, is threatened if not made impossible. The entire weight of decision now rests upon Your shoulders, You have to bear the responsibility for war or peace.

signed: Wilhelm.

Exhibit 23a.

V. The Czar to His Majesty.

Peterhof, July 30th, 1914, 1.20 p. m.

In thank You from my heart for Your quick reply. I am sending to-night Tatisheff (Russian honorary aide to the Kaiser) with instructions. The military measures now taking form were decided upon five days ago, and for the reason of defence against the preparations of Austria. I hope with all my heart that these measures will not influence in any manner Your position as mediator which I appraise very highly. We need Your strong pressure upon Austria so that an understanding can be arrived at with us.

Nicolas.

Exhibit 24.

Telegram of the Chancellor to the Imperial Ambassador at St. Petersburg on July 31st, 1914. Urgent.

In spite of negotiations still pending and although we have up to this hour made no preparations for mobilization, Russia has mobilized her entire army and navy, hence also against us. On account of these Russian measures we have been forced, for the safety of the country, to proclaim the threatening state of war, which does not yet imply mobilization. Mobilization, however, is bound to follow if Russia does not stop every measure of war against us and against Austria-Hungary within 12 hours and notifies us definitely to this effect. Please to communicate this at once to M. Sasonow and wire hour of communication.

Exhibit 25.

Telegram of the Chancellor to the Imperial Ambassador in Paris on July 31st, 1914. Urgent.

Russia has ordered mobilization of her entire army and fleet, therefore also against us in spite of our still pending mediation. We have therefore declared the threatening state of war which is bound to be followed by mobilization unless Russia stops within 12 hours all measures of war against us and Austria. Mobilization inevitably implies war. Please ask French Government whether it intends to remain neutral in a Russo-German war. Reply must be made in 18 hours. Wire at once hour of inquiry. Utmost speed necessary.

Exhibit 26.

Telegram of the Chancellor to the Imperial Ambassador in St. Petersburg on August 1st, 12.52 p. m. Urgent.

If the Russian Government gives no satisfactory reply to our demand, Your Excellency will please transmit this afternoon 5 o'clock (mid-European time) the following statement:

„Le Gouvernement Impérial s'est efforcé dès les débuts de la crise de la mener à une solution pacifique. Se rendant à un désir que lui en avait été exprimé par Sa Majesté l'Empereur de Russie, Sa Majesté l'Empereur d'Allemagne d'accord avec l'Angleterre était appliqué à accomplir un rôle médiateur auprès des Cabinets de Vienne et de St. Pétersbourg, lorsque la Russie, sans en attendre le résultat, procéda à la mobilisation de la totalité de ses forces de terre et de mer.

A la suite de cette mesure menaçante motivée par aucun préparatif militaire de la part de l'Allemagne, l'Empire Allemand se trouva vis-à-vis d'un danger grave et imminent. Si le Gouvernement Impérial eût manqué de parer à ce péril il aurait compromis la sécurité et l'existence même de l'Allemagne. Par conséquent le Gouvernement Allemand se vit forcé de s'adresser au Gouvernement de Sa Majesté l'Empereur de toutes les Russies en sistant sur la cessation des dits actes militaires. La Russie ayant refusé de faire droit à cette demande et ayant manifesté par ce refus, que son action était dirigée contre l'Allemagne, j'ai l'honneur d'ordre de mon Gouvernement de faire savoir à Votre Excellence ce qui suit:

Sa Majesté l'Empereur, mon auguste Souverain, au nom de l'Empire relève le défi et Se considère en état de guerre avec la Russie."

Please wire urgent receipt and time of carrying out this instruction by Russian time.

Please ask for Your passports and turn over protection and affairs to the American Embassy.

Exhibit 27.

Telegram of the Imperial Ambassador in Paris to the Chancellor on August 1ˢᵗ, 1.05 p. m.

Upon my repeated definite inquiry whether France would remain neutral in the event of a Russo-German war, the Prime Minister declared that France would do that which her interests dictated.

Milton Keynes UK
Ingram Content Group UK Ltd.
UKHW032346120224
437723UK00008B/827

9 781014 012616